Satires

Satires

Garrett Buhl Robinson

Poet in the Park
In Humanity I see Grace, Beauty and Dignity.
and some
humor too!
New York City

www.PoetinthePark.com

Table of Content

I know I'm ridiculous
and I am okay with it.

the milton machine

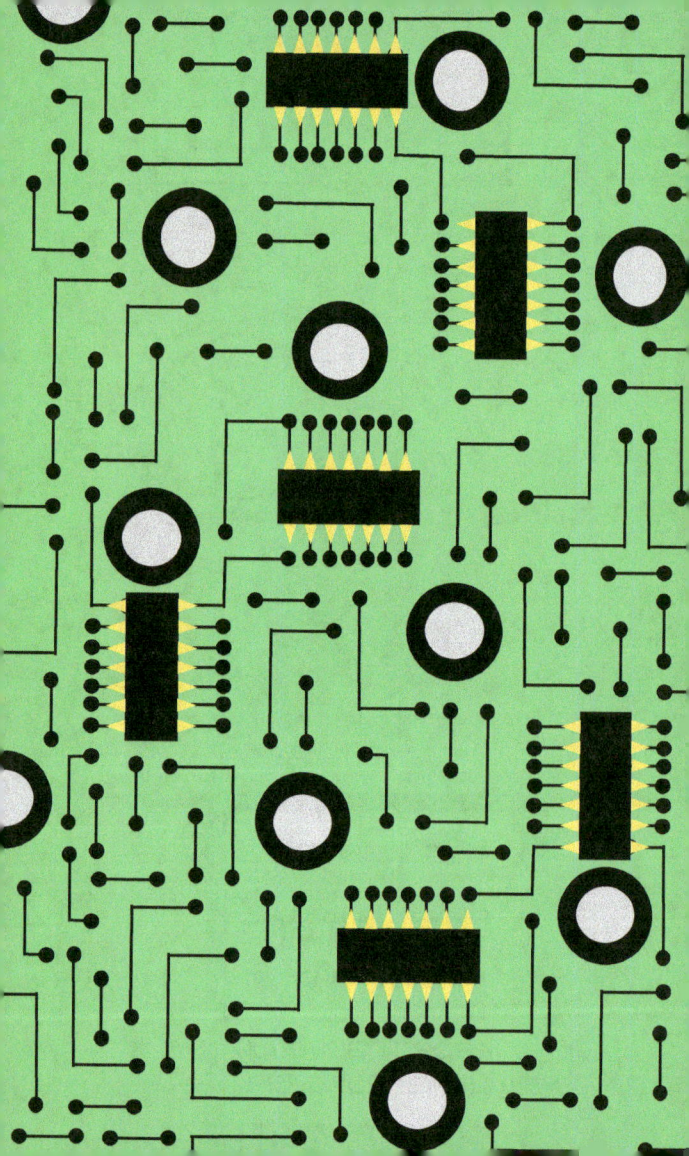

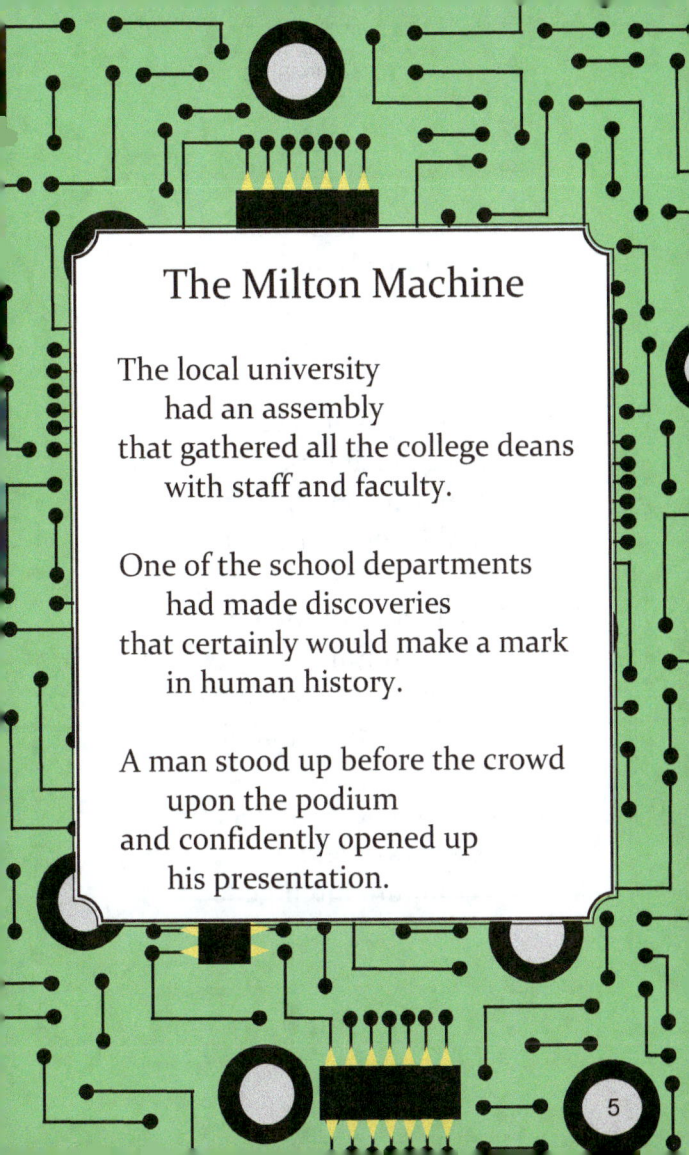

The Milton Machine

The local university
    had an assembly
that gathered all the college deans
    with staff and faculty.

One of the school departments
    had made discoveries
that certainly would make a mark
    in human history.

A man stood up before the crowd
    upon the podium
and confidently opened up
    his presentation.

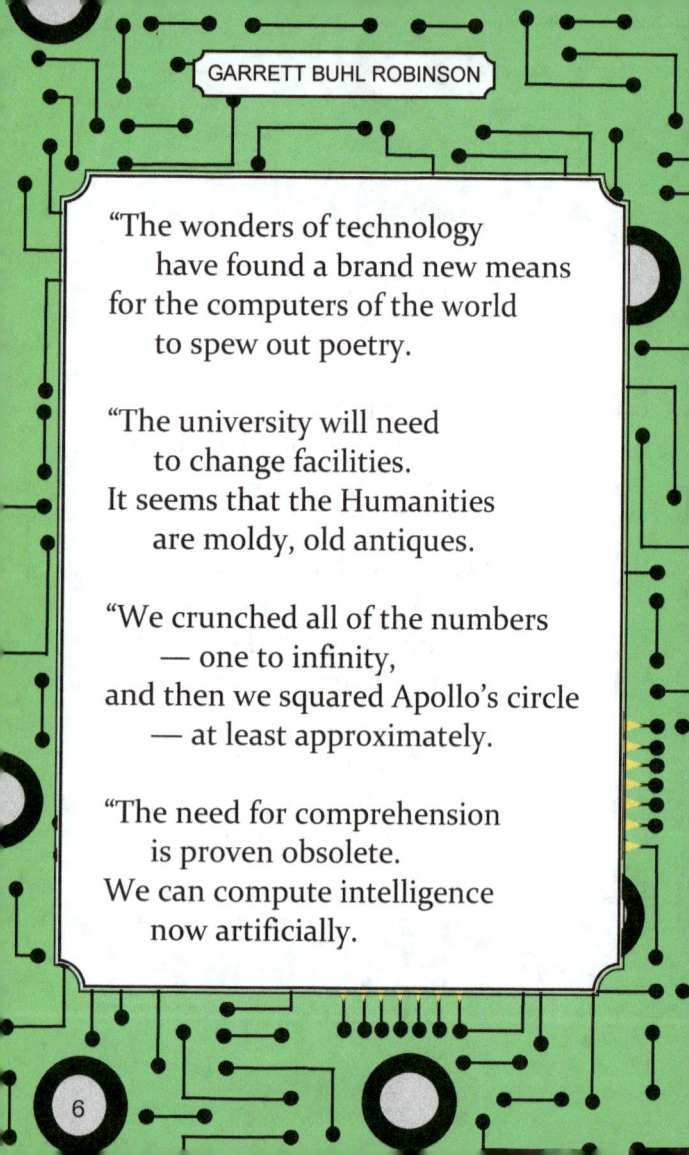

"The wonders of technology
    have found a brand new means
for the computers of the world
    to spew out poetry.

"The university will need
    to change facilities.
It seems that the Humanities
    are moldy, old antiques.

"We crunched all of the numbers
    — one to infinity,
and then we squared Apollo's circle
    — at least approximately.

"The need for comprehension
    is proven obsolete.
We can compute intelligence
    now artificially.

"We'll save a lot of precious time
    with no more books to read
then everyone can spend their funds
    on our technology.

"I thank you all for coming here,
    it seems my work is done,
the fight between the schools of thought
    has finally been won."

One of the deans then took a stand
    to staunchly disagree,
they all had heard this times before
    — it is absurdity.

Maintaining equanimity
    she stood up from her chair
combining solid dignity
    with academic airs.

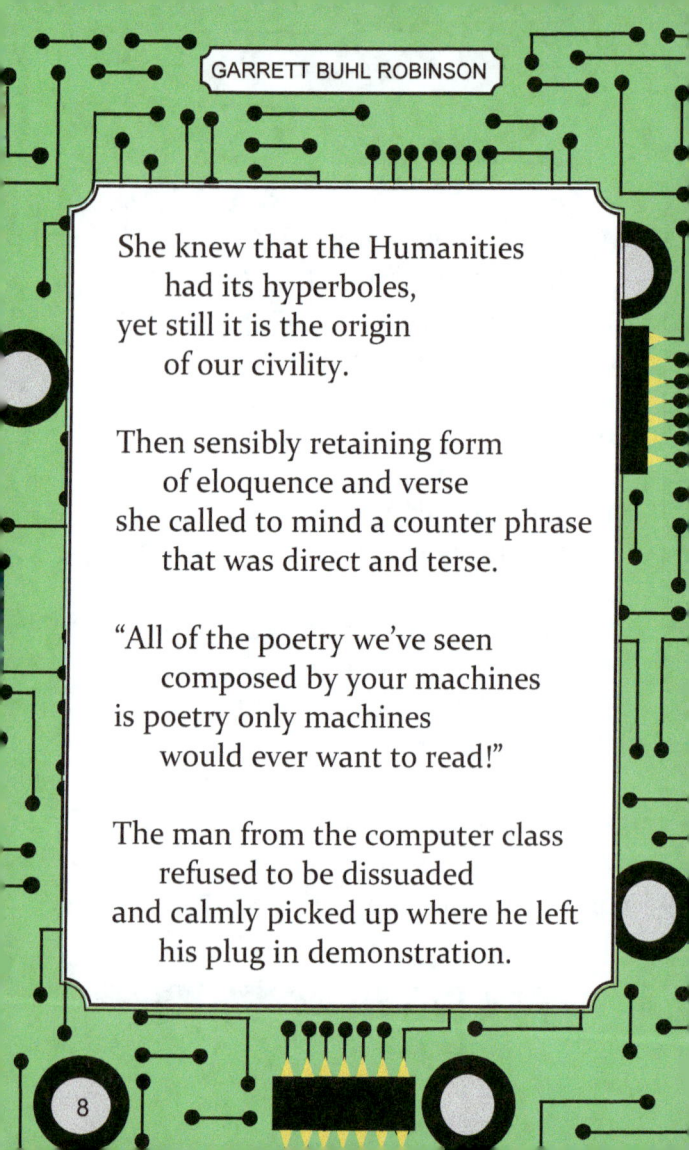

She knew that the Humanities
    had its hyperboles,
yet still it is the origin
    of our civility.

Then sensibly retaining form
    of eloquence and verse
she called to mind a counter phrase
    that was direct and terse.

"All of the poetry we've seen
    composed by your machines
is poetry only machines
    would ever want to read!"

The man from the computer class
    refused to be dissuaded
and calmly picked up where he left
    his plug in demonstration.

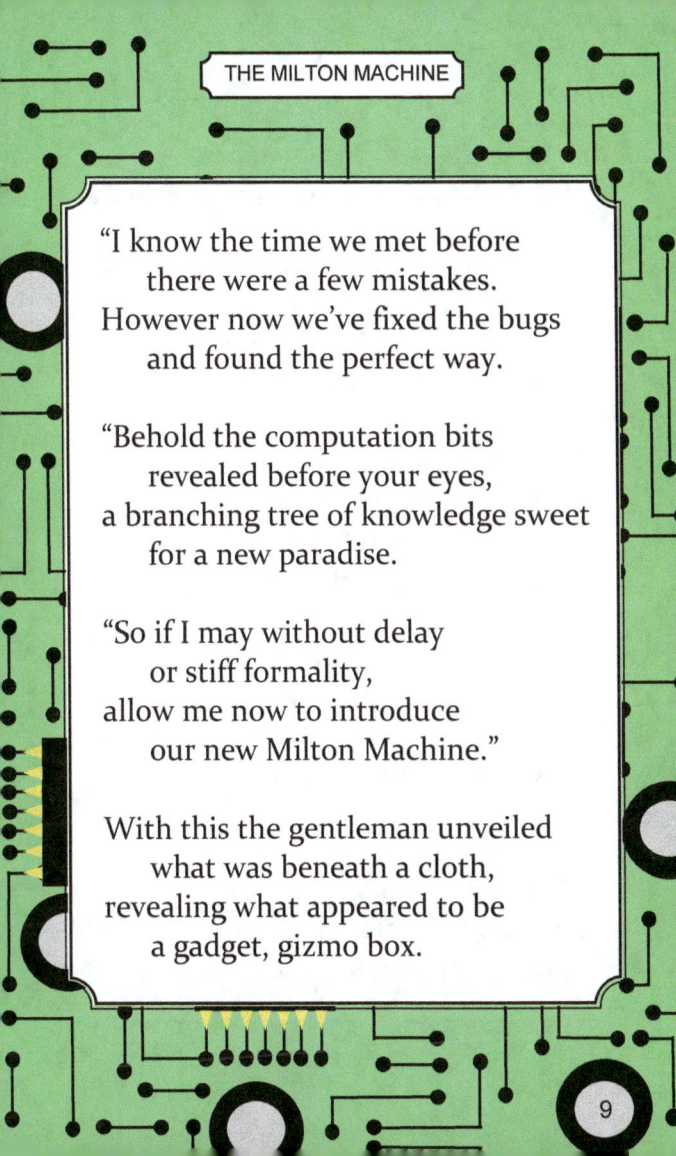

"I know the time we met before
there were a few mistakes.
However now we've fixed the bugs
and found the perfect way.

"Behold the computation bits
revealed before your eyes,
a branching tree of knowledge sweet
for a new paradise.

"So if I may without delay
or stiff formality,
allow me now to introduce
our new Milton Machine."

With this the gentleman unveiled
what was beneath a cloth,
revealing what appeared to be
a gadget, gizmo box.

Then for a change they were amused
    with bathos of theatrics
as he dramatically disclosed
    what looked like a bland package.

But as they paused to scrutinize
    the object on the stage
to all of their astonishment
    they thought they saw a face

— a socket nose and dials for ears,
    each eye a type of gauge,
and then the mouth stuck out a tongue
    of a long printed page.

What was particularly odd,
    although no one confessed,
each thought that the machine looked like
    a disembodied head.

Then oddly in the man's attempt
    to spoil humanity
he inadvertently had made
    pathetic fallacies.

Unveiling the Milton Machine
    he paused the presentation
by making sure they could process
    the stream of information.

Then after a few minutes passed
    he ventured to explain
"Now that you all are interested
    please let me demonstrate."

He flipped a switch on the device
    and it began to reel
and then the sound kept loudening
    as the momentum built.

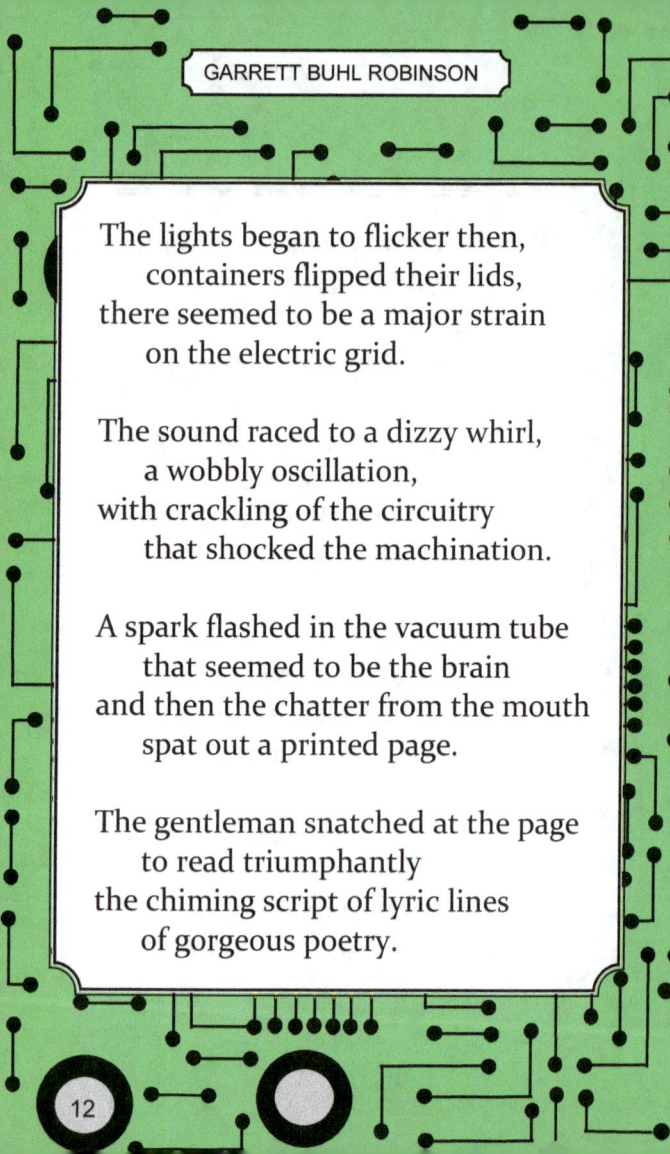

The lights began to flicker then,
    containers flipped their lids,
there seemed to be a major strain
    on the electric grid.

The sound raced to a dizzy whirl,
    a wobbly oscillation,
with crackling of the circuitry
    that shocked the machination.

A spark flashed in the vacuum tube
    that seemed to be the brain
and then the chatter from the mouth
    spat out a printed page.

The gentleman snatched at the page
    to read triumphantly
the chiming script of lyric lines
    of gorgeous poetry.

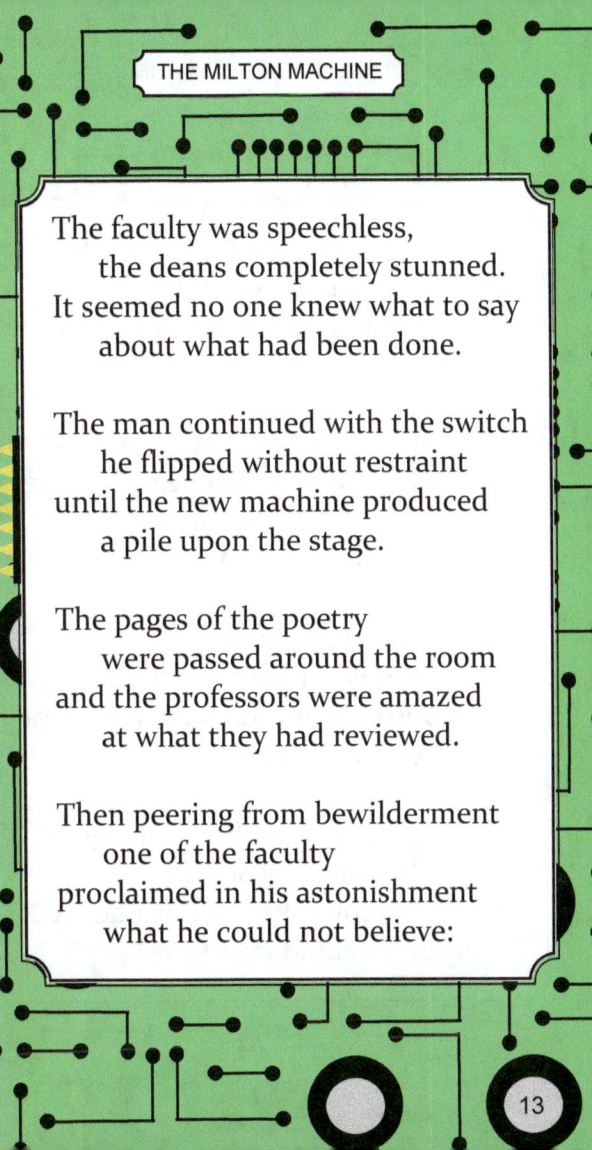

The faculty was speechless,
   the deans completely stunned.
It seemed no one knew what to say
   about what had been done.

The man continued with the switch
   he flipped without restraint
until the new machine produced
   a pile upon the stage.

The pages of the poetry
   were passed around the room
and the professors were amazed
   at what they had reviewed.

Then peering from bewilderment
   one of the faculty
proclaimed in his astonishment
   what he could not believe:

"How could this ever come about?
    How could this ever be?
How can a programmed code achieve
    originality?

"Does this machine possess a mind
    and feel with a real heart?
Or will the MFA's become
    Mass Fabricated Arts?"

The faculty sat vacantly
    as people shook their heads,
then one of them thought to suggest
    a new alternative.

"Perhaps this could be for the good,
    perhaps it's not so bad.
This class could be the most docile
    that we could ever have.

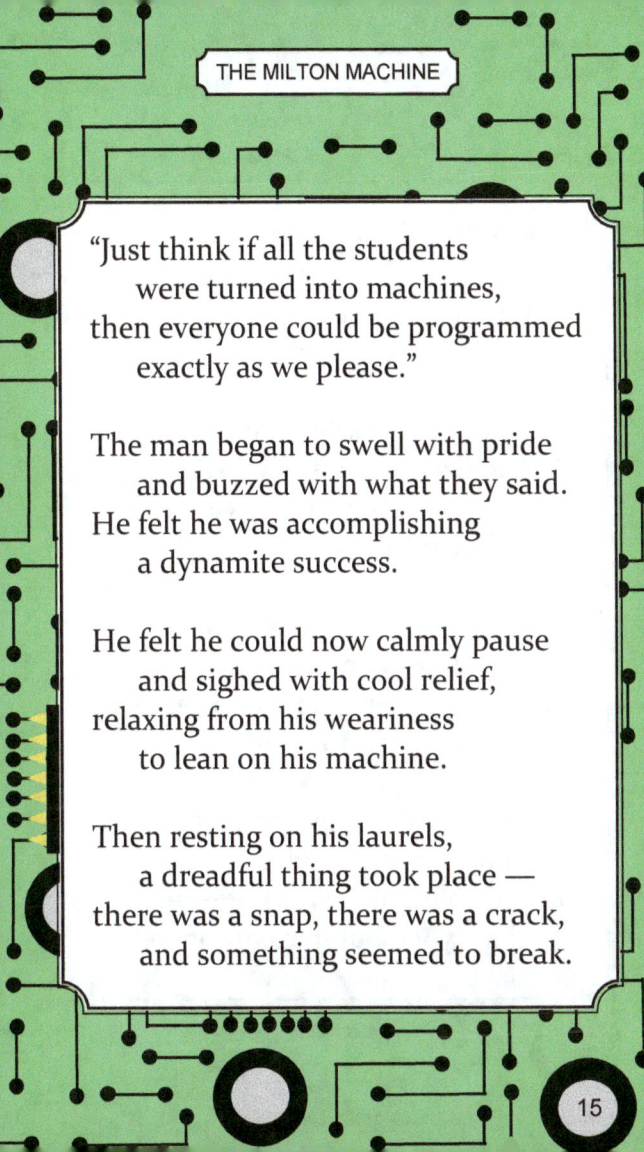

"Just think if all the students
      were turned into machines,
then everyone could be programmed
      exactly as we please."

The man began to swell with pride
      and buzzed with what they said.
He felt he was accomplishing
      a dynamite success.

He felt he could now calmly pause
      and sighed with cool relief,
relaxing from his weariness
      to lean on his machine.

Then resting on his laurels,
      a dreadful thing took place —
there was a snap, there was a crack,
      and something seemed to break.

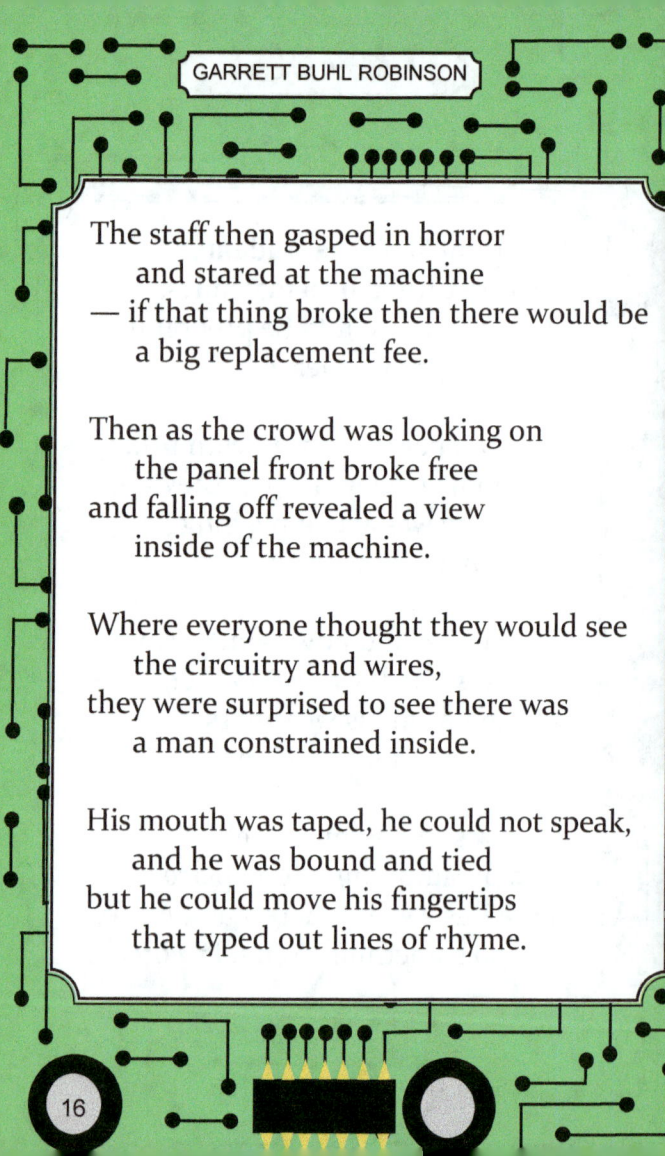

GARRETT BUHL ROBINSON

The staff then gasped in horror
    and stared at the machine
— if that thing broke then there would be
    a big replacement fee.

Then as the crowd was looking on
    the panel front broke free
and falling off revealed a view
    inside of the machine.

Where everyone thought they would see
    the circuitry and wires,
they were surprised to see there was
    a man constrained inside.

His mouth was taped, he could not speak,
    and he was bound and tied
but he could move his fingertips
    that typed out lines of rhyme.

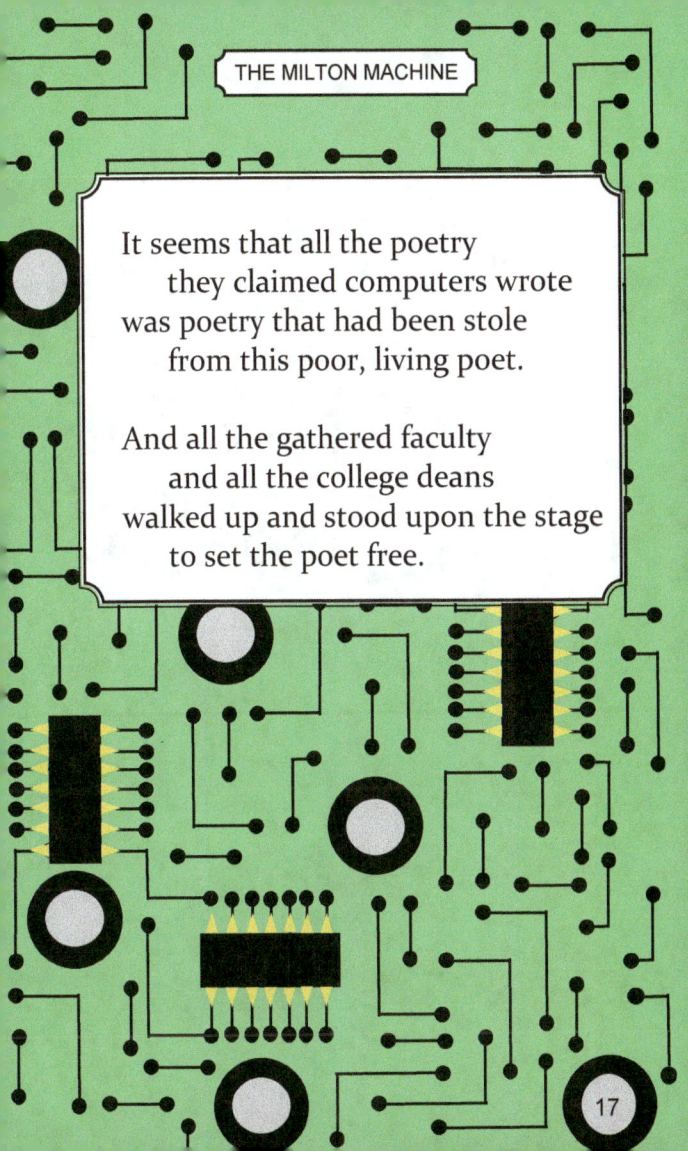

It seems that all the poetry
    they claimed computers wrote
was poetry that had been stole
    from this poor, living poet.

And all the gathered faculty
    and all the college deans
walked up and stood upon the stage
    to set the poet free.

Beauty
and the
Beetle

Beauty and the Beetle
or the clod and the poet

Most would agree a cow pasture
    is not a classic place
for a romantic to reflect
    and write a sweet aubade.

Yet inspiration can arrive
    at unexpected times
and early morning at this place
    I saw the bright sunrise.

Beauty is found in anything
    that's common and is scarce,
and poetry can be composed
    ideally anywhere.

And even in this grassy field
    with tongs of the cowbells
while early morning breezes swirled
    and wafted pungent smells

I could admire the rising sun
    with somber, sullen sighs
and watched the painted clouds that drift
    with colors soaring high.

But then to my astonishment
    directly next to me
I heard a scorn of insolence
    and chiding mockery.

I was content all by myself
    with my delightful dreams
then someone had to spoil the airs
    by ridiculing me.

I brusquely turned around to see
    on top a pile of dung
a merry little beetle laugh
    out loud with loads of fun.

I was surprised that on the dung
    the beetle was so pleased
but I was even more amazed
    when it began to speak.

"You poets are ridiculous
    with all your sappy sighs,
reciting all your mawkish songs
    to clouds up in the sky.

"The greatest beauty of the world
    is right before your feet.
The dung hill I am standing on
    could never be more sweet."

I found this quite incredible
    in two distinctive ways,
was it unreal a beetle spoke
    or was it more his tastes?

I see uplifting lights of dawn
    where spirits may be stirred,
can beauty also plop to ground
    in piles of rank manure?

Then chittering with giggling glee
    it struggled to contain
the beetle shortly calmed again
    and started to explain.

"I often see you poets weep
    in sappy ecstasy,
adoring all the flowery plants
    that kiss the birds and bees.

"You sing about the beautiful
    that's pleasing to the eye
but have you taken any time
    to give a reason why?

"You say that beauty is a vision
    that passes with a flash
and what entrances with allure
    is difficult to grasp.

"You consecrate sublimity
    and shun the practical
as if you seek eternity
    in the ephemeral.

"You say I am a simple bug
    — a beetling, boorish churl,
but dung is the most beautiful
    creation in the world.

"These piles give me a place to live
        and my security,
my sanctuary and my home
        where nothing threatens me.

"There is no fear of an attack
        or an invading force.
I never need to worry here
        or ever lock the doors.

"And with all this it also gives
        the food I love to eat
that cows have carefully prepared
        exclusively for me.

"These piles are always found around
        wherever cattle feed.
They seem to make them naturally
        and give them out for free.

"I've heard your songs of beauty's place
    you yearn and pine to see
but I have always been amazed
    at your perplexity.

"When have you sung of the sweet dung
    where beetles love to live.
We have refinements of our tastes
    that you can't comprehend.

"And singing of the rising sun
    your logic is unsound,
the sun does not rise in the sky
    — the earth is spinning round!

"I hope that you enjoyed to hear
    my lecture on aesthetics.
The next time I will lecture on
    a course of astrophysics."

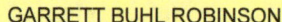

The beetle folded up his wings
    and rested his closed case.
I offered him no argument
    to try to take his place.

Although I was astonished with
    his erudite display,
one lesson I have long since learned
    — don't argue about taste!

The Pond
and the
Palace

The Pond and the Palace

Beneath the pond's reflection of the sky
I see the koi that glide beneath the surface
with lacy fins that swish as they are turning
to nudge and glide in quiet, floating flight.

I must admit I don't know much of them
but guess they are more elderly than me
— they live for longer than two centuries
and glow like painted lanterns as they swim.

I find myself amused to think that they
live in the midst of a metropolis
yet seem to be indifferent to this,
apparently content in their own way.

I'm certain that from all the dribbling streams
that run from off the overflowing streets
they get a twinging taste of the city,
a distant sense of what they may not see.

One breaks the surface for a gulp of air
and for an instant, we exchange a glance,
before the shiny scales of its smooth flank
recede into the deep to disappear.

Then losing sight from the primordial depths
I stroll along the path in the daylight
and then adjust the focus of my sight
to what the surface of the pond reflects.

Then lifting over traffic and the trees
my eyes look up at windows in the sky
that rise into the tiered majestic heights
of the grand Palace soaring by the street.

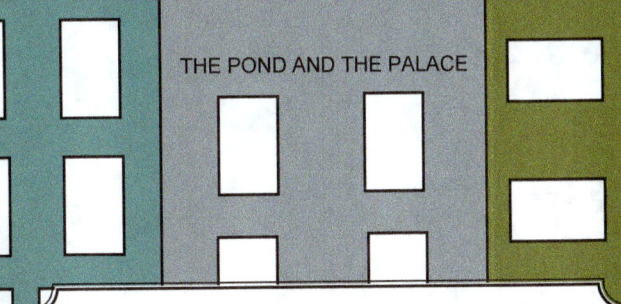

Then suddenly I am surprised to see
a figure standing solemnly alone
inside one of the Palace's windows
while holding up a crystal glass of drink.

Perhaps it is a solipsistic notion
but for a moment I pause to believe
that person in the window gazed at me
within the stillness of a deep reflection.

Then there is something that is understood
for the bright glance when we make eye contact
before he turns and suddenly walks back
into the privacy of his abode.

Standing

at

Attention

Standing at Attention

I can recall one day before closed quarters
in military school's strict, rigid orders,
all us cadets were waiting in our rooms
for study hours precisely to resume.
During the pause I had a jar of soap
and dipped the ring where bubbles could be blown
and launched a cloud of little pristine globes
that drifted in the quad out my window.

Then suddenly the Commandant approached.
I closed the window quick before he'd know
and at attention by my desk inside
I peeked out of the corner of my eye
for the response the Commandant would make
expecting him to burst into a rage
and then demand the culprit to confess
as an outrageous insubordinate
— The discipline of military school
is not the place for silly clowns and fools!

But then to my amazement and surprise
I saw the Commandant pause for a while
to watch the gentle bubbles floating by
and then I saw the hint of a kind smile
and when the lofty bubbles all had passed
he then resumed his firm and purposed path.

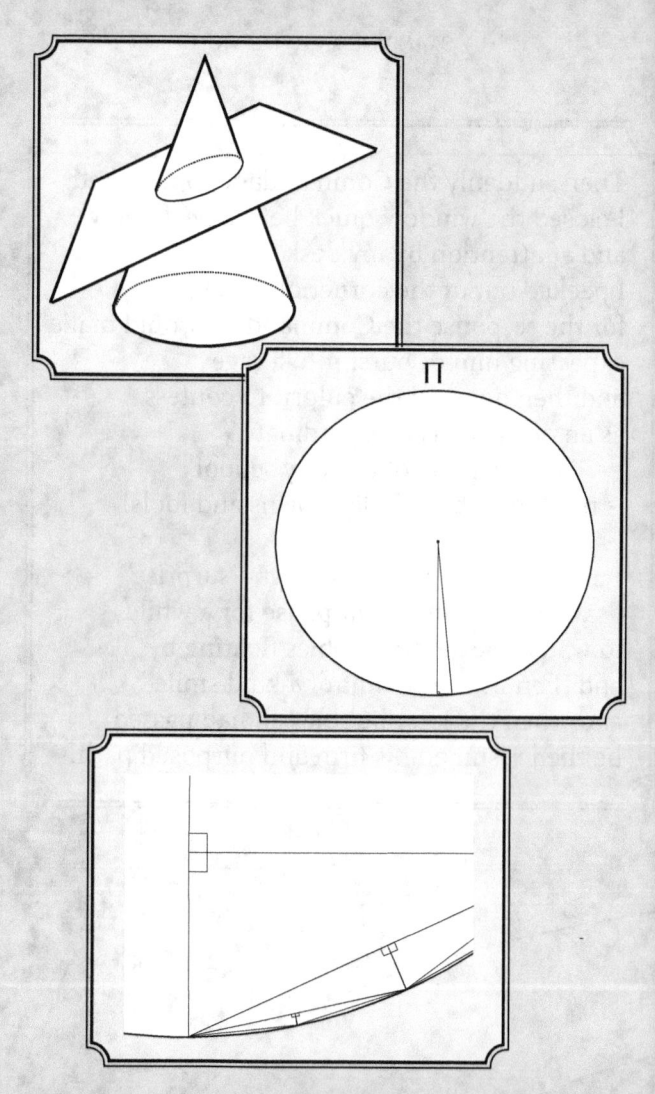

A Classic Lesson

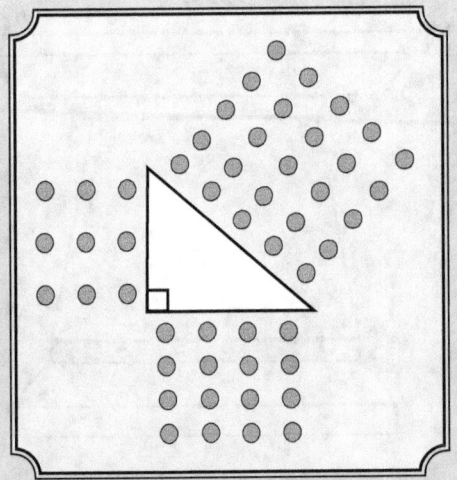

A Classic Lesson

Wise Aristotle was perplexed
  and brought to his wit's end
when he agreed that he would teach
  and tutor a king's kid.

The king of Macedonia
  had paid a hefty sum
for Aristotle to instruct
  and educate his son.

We know his son as Alexander,
  a very strong willed boy,
and he remains esteemed as great
  for his renowned exploits.

Yet he grew up with challenges
   despite his royalty
and could not grasp the elements
   to learn geometry.

And even though the famous sage
   explained the universe
with eloquent elucidations
   of his exacting words,

he was not able to explain
   for his pupil to learn
that education only comes
   through concentrated work.

And pacing back and forth he'd say,
   "To learn geometry
there is no magic, golden road.
   You must learn how to think.

"It does not matter who you are,
   your creed or wealth or state,
if you desire to understand
   then you must concentrate."

So Aristotle made a point
   to carefully outline
to try to make the lessons plain
   before his pupil's eyes.

He made a center with a stick
   then with a measured string
drew out a circle's graceful arc
   so that the ends would meet.

He then explained the elegance,
   the symmetry and grace,
the ratio and measurement
   of this proportioned shape.

He said no matter what the size,
  the time or place or space,
there are the common properties
  in every circle made.

And Aristotle then explained
  how the diameter
is equal with a ratio
  to the circumference turn

and that the measured ratio
  is known for all of time
as the valued identity
  that is expressed as Pi.

Then Alexander snuffed and asked
  "Exactly what is Pi?
You must give me something exact.
  What is the bottom line?"

Then Aristotle cleaned the slate
  "The number is transcendent
— it goes on for infinity
  beyond a definition.

"There is no pattern that we know
  or end we recognize,
but searching is exactly how
  precision is refined.

"So in the measurements we make
  with careful calculations,
we are developing ourselves
  by aiming at perfection."

"But if it is impossible"
  young Alexander asked,
"then what is worth the effort then?
  It is a futile task!"

Then Aristotle clarified,
    "It's not in what's obtained.
The true development in life
    is how we are engaged.

"Perfection is a pure ideal,
    a place we cannot reach,
that's how it is a path that leads
    into infinity."

Then Aristotle introduced
    a nifty formula
that was developed at the school
    of wise Pythagoras.

He showed how right triangle sides
    could always be inferred
— the length of two is all one needs
    to calculate the third.

Then following the process through
    to make the calculation,
the answer could always be reached
    with the correct summation.

Then Alexander pertly said
    that he was not amused.
He then demanded an account
    for the square root of two.

Then Aristotle shook his head,
    he was too wise to shout,
but did not know what could be made
    of the irrational.

And then the wise instructor said,
    "Plato's Academy
was closed to those who did not know
    any geometry.

"For any new development
 you must build a foundation.
All structures will collapse and fall
 if you neglect the basis.

"Geometry is the sure way
 for measuring the world.
We need defining disciplines
 to which we can refer."

Then Alexander stomped his feet
 and threw a royal fit —
"Why bother measuring the world
 when I will conquer it!"

Then Aristotle was distressed
 and looked to be displeased.
He was a student of Plato
 who learned from Socrates.

It is one matter to acquire,
  another to sustain,
and this may emphasize the need
  for building a firm base.

And although Alexander made
  an empire stretched out far,
it was not measured carefully
  and quickly fell apart.

Presentations
of Poetry

Presentations of Poetry

There was a public gathering
    for thoughtful inquiry
— the local intellectuals
    and scholars with degrees.

They gathered with a cultured group
    and college faculty
to hear two lectures to be read
    inside the library.

The lecturers were of renown
    with academic seats,
with high regard within their field
    — the art of poetry.

With lectures carefully prepared
    upon a certain theme
they planned to offer new insight
    with their authority

to celebrate respectfully
    the valued legacy
of Whitman's great accomplishments
    and anniversary.

Then following each scholar's speech
    they'd read from their own verse
so closings of the lecturing
    would open with new work.

So all the people in attendance
    filed in the rows of seats
while murmuring in eagerness
    with folded program leaves.

And placed beside the podium
    while waiting to be called
the speakers sat with patience
    inside the lecture hall.

Then following the opening
    with brief biographies
the first guest speaker was announced
    with a warm welcoming.

And wearing the expected tweed
    — a scholar's token coat
for sitting at a scholar's desk
    and patched at the elbows —

a gentleman stood with his name
    announced before the crowd
and he appeared fully prepared
    both confident and proud.

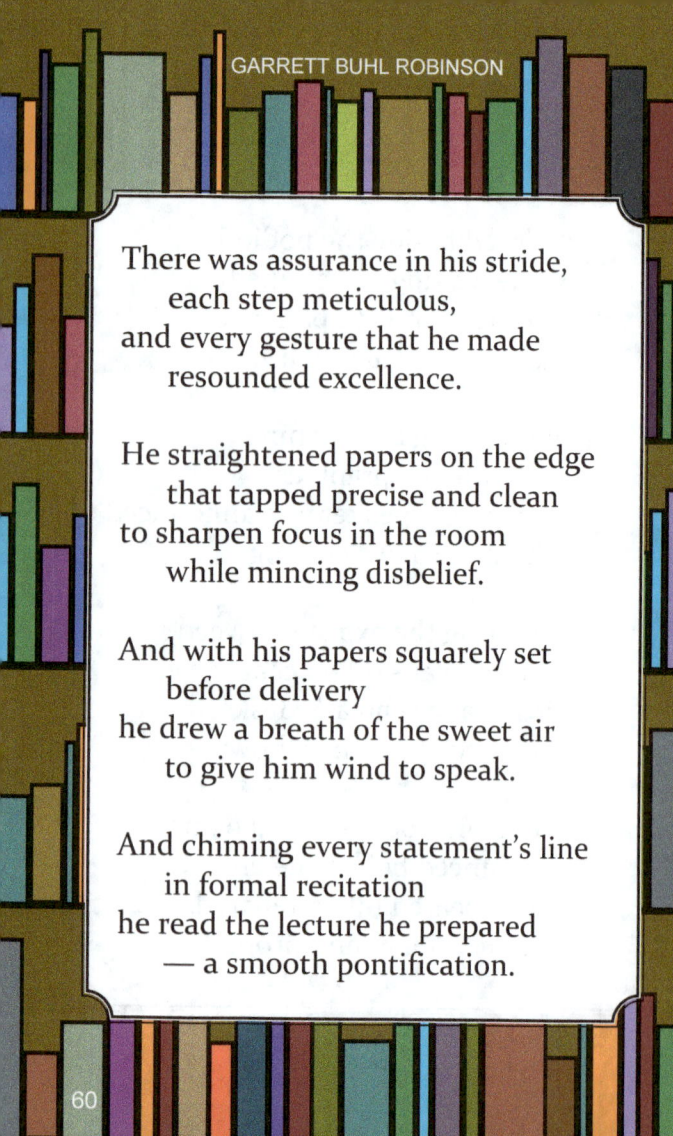

There was assurance in his stride,
    each step meticulous,
and every gesture that he made
    resounded excellence.

He straightened papers on the edge
    that tapped precise and clean
to sharpen focus in the room
    while mincing disbelief.

And with his papers squarely set
    before delivery
he drew a breath of the sweet air
    to give him wind to speak.

And chiming every statement's line
    in formal recitation
he read the lecture he prepared
    — a smooth pontification.

And he did more than just explain,
    he served to lead a journey
where every person could explore
    the poet's territory.

He guided people on each step
    to climb the lyric lines
so poems served as flights of stairs
    to elevate the mind.

And then upon the dizzy heights
    of each conclusion made
he opened up the panoramas
    of cultural landscapes.

And as he explicated poems,
    revealing their bright light,
he showed how they could serve as lanterns
    illuminating life.

Some poems could be vehicles
    and others served as maps,
topographies of the terrain
    for each to find a path.

Some poems offer exercise
    for vigor of one's thought
while giving insight and ideas
    for minds both tone and taut.

And the poetic inquiry
    prepared them for surprise
so they could earnestly maintain
    dexterity of mind

as poems open new frontiers
    to grow imagination
with bridges over obstacles
    with new associations.

Then summoning the mythical
    a centaur then appeared
and as the lecturer explained
    they saw the image clear.

And trotting right into the hall
    the centaur drew his bow
and with the sinews stretched out tight
    he let the arrow go

and arcing in the vision's distance
    the arrow struck its mark
and then the centaur calmly turned
    to trot off and depart.

And everyone sat struck with awe
    before the orator,
the lecture that he gave seemed like
    a classic music score.

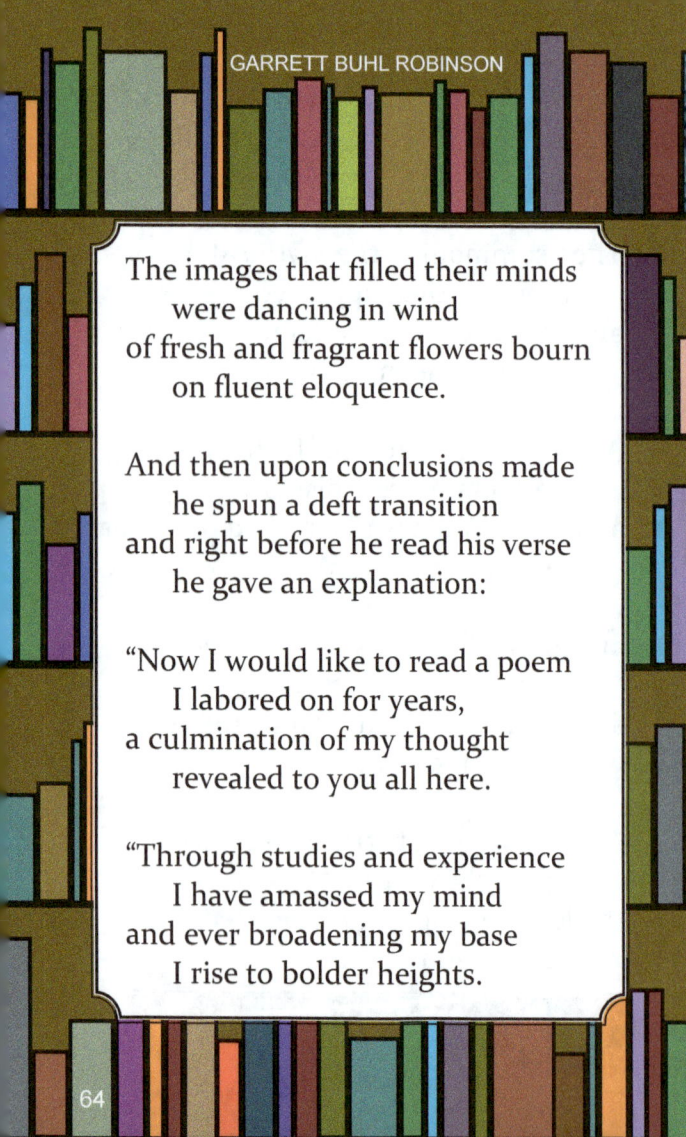

The images that filled their minds
        were dancing in wind
of fresh and fragrant flowers bourn
        on fluent eloquence.

And then upon conclusions made
        he spun a deft transition
and right before he read his verse
        he gave an explanation:

"Now I would like to read a poem
        I labored on for years,
a culmination of my thought
        revealed to you all here.

"Through studies and experience
        I have amassed my mind
and ever broadening my base
        I rise to bolder heights.

"But this is more than just a mass
    precariously piled,
it must be structured orderly
   with erudite design.

"So I composed a work of verse
   evoking the profound
to set upon my whole life's work
   — a culminating crown.

"The first point everyone will note
   — the poem has no title,
because it cannot be defined
   by silly, little labels.

"For any poem to have worth
   it needs no explanation.
Magnificence is only said
   through its own proclamation.

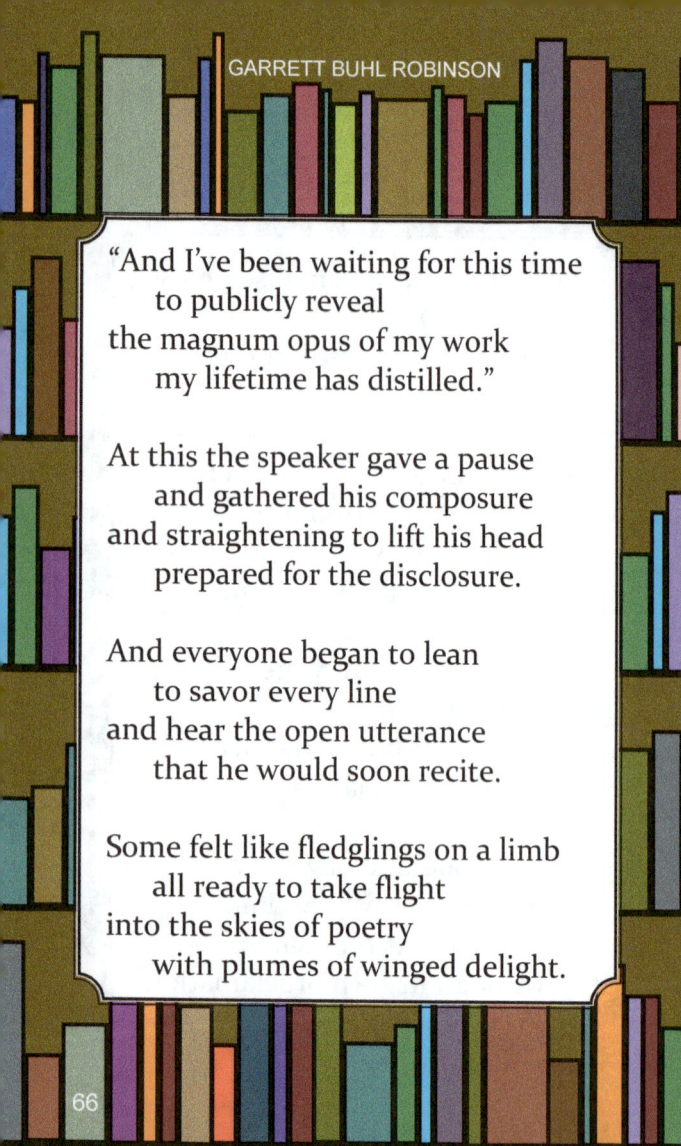

"And I've been waiting for this time
　　to publicly reveal
the magnum opus of my work
　　my lifetime has distilled."

At this the speaker gave a pause
　　and gathered his composure
and straightening to lift his head
　　prepared for the disclosure.

And everyone began to lean
　　to savor every line
and hear the open utterance
　　that he would soon recite.

Some felt like fledglings on a limb
　　all ready to take flight
into the skies of poetry
　　with plumes of winged delight.

Some felt that they were at the sea
    and standing on the beach
preparing vessels to be launched
    for new discoveries.

Some felt they climbed a mountainside
    and scaled the granite steep
and they were on the verge to cap
    the mountain's lofty peak.

Although in their own metaphors
    they tacitly agreed
that they all stood at the threshold
    of lyric majesty.

And as if lightning lit the room
    the lecturer then spoke:
"I watch the water pass below
    the railing of the boat."

At this they felt they all might fall
    through their expectancy
that seemed to be confronted with
    a chilling vacancy.

They all were thrilled when they had heard
    the poetry begin
but in the joyful opening
    it came to a quick end.

A power lies in poetry's
    ambiguous suggestion
but they had hoped for something more
    than just a vague impression.

The flowing fabric of the night
    frayed with anxiety
as both the speaker and the group
    stayed in expectancy.

The crowd anticipated more
from this suspenseful pause.
The speaker waited patiently
expecting an applause.

Well skilled as a strict pedagogue
the speaker then instructed:
"This is the time that clapping hands
is normally conducted."

And scattered in perplexity
some people clapped their hands
and then the others joined along
to patronize the man.

And then the speaker quickly turned
and walked back to his station
at where he sat upon the stage
before he lost his patience.

When the next speaker was announced
    she stumbled at the door
as when she stood her papers spilled
    and dumped upon the floor.

Her blouse was skewed and buttoned wrong,
    she wore a rumpled dress,
her hair was frizzy and unpinned
    and looked to be a mess.

She scrambled for her scattered leaves
    as others tried to help
and shared the sore embarrassment
    although they all meant well.

The other speaker helped her out
    and seemed compassionate
but he was loath to be around
    such gross incompetence.

Then as she sorted jumbled sheets
     upon the podium
the audience sat witnessing
     the pandemonium.

She puzzled over crumpled leaves
     she scattered on the floor
and seemed as if she never had
     looked at the speech before.

Then sorting through her printed speech
     she mashed the papers flat
as if she hoped she could conceal
     a pile beneath a matt.

She then let out an anguished sigh
     with difficulties done
although the worst calamities
     had still not yet begun.

Then reading her soliloquy
    for everyone to hear
she turned a page but was dismayed
    — no second page was there!

But even with a frantic search
    it seemed that she had lost it
so she gave a quick summery
    to touch upon the topics.

And then she picked up at page three
    where she resumed to read
but often edited herself
    while she was lecturing.

It's not that she was unprepared,
    she works in privacy,
and draws upon her deep set well
    of sensitivity.

The public always tugs and shoves
    and forces her off course
and each professional mandate
    can bump her out of sorts.

Yet staggering she manages
    to do another chore
to recompose and give her speech
    that spilled upon the floor.

Arriving at the lecture's end
    she felt a sense of doubt
with murmurs of perplexity
    in the crestfallen crowd.

But suddenly the spirits rose
    with sighs of sweet relief
at the first chance that she could do
    what she does naturally.

GARRETT BUHL ROBINSON

And everyone became entranced
    with gentle, lilting lines
and listened to her poetry
    resplendently divine.

She seemed to sing from a top stem
    that kissed the clear blue sky
awakening a brilliant day
    with music in each line.

The grand achievements rhymed each time
    and radiated light
while deftly dancing metric steps
    with phrases filled with life.

And everyone was held in awe
    with the sweet touch of verse
and felt to levitate within
    the bliss of what they heard.

Garrett Buhl Robinson is a poet living in New York City. Originally from Alabama, he has lived at numerous places across the United States while studying intensely, writing prolifically and supporting himself with odd jobs.

In 2011, he moved to New York City with the intent to find a publisher. Unable to reach anyone, he began selling his books on the streets in 2012. He has since established his own publishing company - Poet in the Park.

Most days, he can be found at his wobbly, little bookstand in Midtown Manhattan where he recites his poetry to the public.

He is privy to a special New York City secret too — everyone knows about dollar slices of cheese pizza, but he knows places where you can get a dollar slice of pizza with four free toppings! — Yeah! Salt, pepper, Parmesan cheese and hot sauce!

Some other titles by Garrett Buhl Robinson

<u>Poetry</u>
Pilgrims
Whispering Emily
The Ballad of Emperor Norton
City of Poems
A Man Who Lives in a Dream
Little Pieces of Poetry
The Nobody
Beauty beyond Reason
Martha, a poem

<u>Fiction</u>
Zoë
Nunatak

Poet in the Park ®
In Humanity I see Grace, Beauty and Dignity
New York City

www.PoetinthePark.com